SPOTLIGHT ON NATIVE AMERICANS

CHEYENNE

Terra Rose Maron

PowerKiDS
press.

New York

Published in 2016 by The Rosen Publishing Group, Inc.
29 East 21st Street, New York, NY 10010

First Edition

Editor: Karolena Bielecki
Book Design: Kris Everson
Reviewed by: Robert J. Conley, Former Sequoyah Distinguished Professor at Western Carolina University and Director of Native American Studies at Morningside College and Montana State University
Supplemental material reviewed by: Donald A. Grinde, Jr., Professor of Transnational/American Studies at the State University of New York at Buffalo.

Photo credits: Cover Universal Images Group/Getty Images; pp. 4–5 © iStockphoto.com/ brown54486; pp. 7, 8, 9, 11 Peter Newark's American Pictures; pp. 12, 17 (both), 18, 19, 21 (right), 25, 27 Native Stock; pp. 14, 21 (left) Corbis; p. 15 © iStockphoto.com/duncan1890; p. 23 Paul J. Richards/AFP/Getty Images; p. 28 Bill Koplitz/FEMA Photo Library/Wikimedia; p. 29 © iStockphoto.com/ David Parsons.

Library of Congress Cataloging-in-Publication Data

Maron, Terra Rose.
 Cheyenne / Terra Rose Maron.
    pages cm. — (Spotlight on Native Americans)
 Includes bibliographical references and index.
 ISBN 978-1-4994-1676-3 (pbk.)
 ISBN 978-1-4994-1675-6 (6 pack)
 ISBN 978-1-4994-1678-7 (library binding)
 1. Cheyenne Indians—History—Juvenile literature. 2. Cheyenne Indians—Social life and customs—Juvenile literature. I. Title.
 E99.C53M32 2016
 978.004'97353—dc23
                                                              2015007809

Manufactured in the United States of America

CPSIA Compliance Information: Batch #WS15PK: For Further Information contact Rosen Publishing, New York, New York at 1-800-237-9932

CONTENTS

THE CHEYENNE LANDS

CHAPTER 1

The Cheyennes are a North American native people who became one of the most famous tribes of the Great Plains during the nineteenth century. Today, about 8,000 Northern Cheyennes live on the Northern Cheyenne **Reservation** in Montana. About 5,000 Southern Cheyennes live in Oklahoma, mostly on or near the Concho Reservation, which they share with the Southern Arapaho tribe.

A Cheyenne in **powwow** dress at the Red Earth Festival. This large competitive powwow is held each June in downtown Oklahoma City.

The Cheyennes' name for themselves is *Tsetschestahase,* meaning "people who are alike" or "our people." The name *Cheyenne* derives from a Sioux word, *Shai-ena,* meaning "people of an **alien** speech."

No one knows exactly how the Cheyennes and other Native American peoples came to North

America, but like many cultures, traditional Cheyennes explain their arrival in an origin story. According to this story, all things were formed by a Creator, who made three kinds of people in the far north—hairy people, white people, and red people. The red people followed the hairy people to the south, but the hairy people eventually disappeared. When the red people returned to the north, they found that the white people were gone. The Creator then gave the red people corn to grow and buffalo to hunt.

Buffalo grazing in Montana

FROM WOODLANDS TO GREAT PLAINS

CHAPTER 2

For hundreds of years, the Cheyennes were a woodland people living in the Great Lakes region in permanent villages. Their lifestyle, based on hunting, fishing, and farming, was similar to that of other woodland peoples.

During the early 1700s, however, the Cheyennes were driven west to the northern Great Plains south of today's Canada by their enemies, the Assiniboins and Ojibwes, and became **nomadic** buffalo hunters. There they met the Sutaio tribe, a people so closely related to them they could understand each others' language. By about 1800, the Sutaios had joined the Cheyenne tribe. The Cheyennes acquired horses from other Native American groups around 1760, becoming much more mobile. They were able to follow the buffalo herds, becoming a mighty Great Plains tribe.

During the early 1800s, however, American traders brought **whiskey** to exchange with the Cheyennes for

Hunting buffaloes on horseback was dangerous work requiring great skill. Horses, however, allowed hunters to cover more ground and kill more buffaloes.

their buffalo robes. **Alcoholism** became a big problem for the tribe.

By 1832, the Cheyenne tribe had separated into Northern Cheyennes, who lived mainly in northern Wyoming and southeastern Montana, and Southern Cheyennes, who stayed mainly in the Arkansas and North Canadian River valleys in eastern Colorado, southwestern Kansas, and northwestern Oklahoma.

WAR ON THE SOUTHERN PLAINS

CHAPTER 3

In 1849, the U.S. Army established Fort Laramie in eastern Wyoming to protect American settlers traveling on the Oregon Trail. Cheyennes and many other Plains tribes signed the Fort Laramie **Treaty** of 1851, allowing safe passage of the **immigrants**.

In 1856, peaceful Cheyennes were fired at on the Oregon Trail in Nebraska. The Cheyennes wounded the

Colonel John Chivington led the Sand Creek Massacre.

wagon driver with an arrow. In revenge, soldiers from Fort Kearney, Nebraska, killed eight Cheyenne. The incident ignited a war that would last until the 1880s.

Southern Cheyenne leader, Chief Black Kettle, tried to pursue peace. However, the Colorado Volunteer **Militia**, led by Colonel John Chivington, attacked Black Kettle's

A second Treaty of Fort Laramie was signed in 1868. Here, U.S. treaty commissioners are shown with chiefs of the Cheyenne and Arapaho tribes.

peaceful village in eastern Colorado in 1864, an event called the Sand Creek **Massacre**.

The 1867 Treaty of Medicine Lodge, signed by the Southern Cheyennes, the Kiowas, Arapahos, and Comanches, was the federal government's first attempt to confine the Plains tribes to reservations. Just a year later, Lieutenant Colonel George Armstrong Custer and the U.S. Seventh Cavalry surprise attacked Black Kettle's village and killed many Cheyennes, including Black Kettle and his wife. By 1869, the Southern Cheyennes were forced to move to a reservation in Indian Territory in what is now Oklahoma.

WAR ON THE NORTHERN PLAINS

CHAPTER 4

Meanwhile, the Northern Cheyennes, led by Little Wolf and Dull Knife, joined the Lakota Sioux, led by Red Cloud, in the war over the Bozeman Trail in the 1860s. Together, the Indians forced the U.S. Army to abandon the trail to Montana and the three army forts that had been built to protect gold miners who were **trespassing** on Cheyenne and Lakota land.

During the 1870s, Northern Cheyennes again joined the Lakotas in war. The 1868 Treaty of Fort Laramie gave the Black Hills of South Dakota to the Cheyennes and Lakotas as their sacred lands. When gold was discovered there in 1874, however, the U.S. government sent troops to protect the prospectors who took the land for their own. In June 1876, Northern Cheyennes and Lakotas shocked U.S. generals invading Cheyenne homelands by turning back the army at the Battle of the Rosebud and wiping out the Seventh Cavalry at the Battle of the Little Bighorn. By the late 1870s, however, the army had forced all the Plains Indians to accept reservation life.

Cheyenne chiefs Dull Knife (seated) and Little Wolf were part of the war waged over the Bozeman Trail in 1877. It remains one of the only wars that the United States ever lost.

FORCED ONTO RESERVATIONS

CHAPTER 5

By 1869, the Southern Cheyennes had been forced to share a reservation in western Indian Territory with the Southern Arapahos. There, they endured **poverty** and sickness and were forced to adopt white values. Their religious beliefs were suppressed. Their children attended boarding schools.

This photo from 1889 shows Cheyennes and Arapahos on their reservation in Indian Territory near Fort Reno.

The U.S. government forced the Northern Cheyennes to move to the Southern Cheyenne reservation, promising they could return to their northern homelands if they didn't like the reservation. The largest group, 937 people, arrived in August 1877. Within two months, two-thirds of them were sick with an illness called malaria.

The government denied the Northern Cheyennes' request to return home. In 1878, a large group of Cheyennes left anyway. The army killed many during their journey, but about 200 reached their old homes. In 1884, a presidential order created the Northern Cheyenne Reservation in southeastern Montana and allowed these Cheyennes to remain.

During the 1880s, the U.S. government forced the Southern Cheyennes to divide their shared land into small plots (a process called **allotment**). In 1892, their remaining 3.5 million acres (1.4 million ha) were opened to white settlers. Northern Cheyennes, however, kept control of most of their land. Today, the tribe still owns nearly 97 percent of its reservation.

TRADITIONAL CHEYENNE LIFE

CHAPTER 6

In the Great Lakes woodlands where the tribe first lived, the Cheyennes farmed, fished, and hunted. There, they also made pottery, an art that was lost when they were forced to move to the Great Plains.

When the Cheyennes acquired horses in about 1760, their way of life on the Plains changed dramatically. Before the arrival of horses, Cheyenne camps, including **tepees**, were moved on small sleds, called travois, made of poles and dragged by dogs. Horses could pull a much larger travois, so tepees could be a lot bigger.

A Southern Cheyenne family in 1890 uses a horse travois to pull their belongings.

Horses also made buffalo hunting much easier and more productive. Hunters could travel farther and faster in search of buffaloes. With more food, children died less frequently, allowing the Cheyennes to grow into a large and powerful tribe. The Cheyennes also became an important link in the chain of horse-trading that made horses readily available to tribes throughout the Great Plains region. Stealing horses from other tribes was also considered a great sport.

This engraving from the 1880s shows a Cheyenne encampment.

GROWING UP CHEYENNE

CHAPTER 7

Family life has always been very important to the Cheyenne people. In traditional Cheyenne communities, children are surrounded by relatives of all ages and by elders who take a special interest in the children.

This did not mean, however, that the children were limited in what they could do. On the Great Plains, Cheyenne children were given great freedom and allowed to make decisions for themselves almost as though they were adults. This was especially true regarding horse riding. From a very early age, Cheyenne boys and girls practically grew up on horseback, becoming amazingly skilled long before they were teenagers.

Around the Cheyenne camps, young boys played with small bows and arrows, shooting at birds. Girls had dolls made by their grandmothers and played house with small tepees that were only about knee-high.

When it was time to get married, Cheyenne **courtship** could last as long as five years before the girl would agree to marry. A girl's family arranged some marriages,

(Left) A Cheyenne cradleboard allowed a mother to work while her baby remained safe. *(Right)* By carrying the baby on her back, a Cheyenne mother could keep her hands free for other work.

but many also developed out of dating and courtship. Dating always took place under the watchful eyes of her relatives.

GOVERNMENT AND SOCIETIES

CHAPTER 8

The Cheyennes were famous for their Council of Forty-Four, which originally consisted of four chiefs from each of the 11 Cheyenne bands. Its main role was to settle disputes among the people. Over time, the number of bands decreased. Some entire bands were lost during an **epidemic** in 1849. However, the Cheyennes maintained the council tradition.

Porcupine quills, some of them dyed, decorated clothing and other items.

Nearly every Cheyenne man belonged to a society, which were like military and social clubs. The Dog Soldier Society became probably the most famous warriors on the Great Plains in the 1800s. These brave and skilled fighters were among the greatest **light cavalry** in the history of warfare. They led all other Cheyenne warriors into battle. When the tribe moved its camp, they were the rear guard.

Being invited to join the Dog Soldier Society was one of the highest honors a Cheyenne warrior could achieve.

Cheyenne women had their own societies. Membership in the Quillers' Society was a high honor. They maintained high standards in making the most elaborate clothing decorated with porcupine quills and for instructing young women in the craft.

The most remarkable Cheyenne society was the Contraries. Its members were required to do most things the opposite of how other people did them. Walking backward and saying good-bye when you meant hello was not a routine that everyone could learn how to do.

BELIEFS

CHAPTER 9

The Cheyennes believe in a Creator and an afterlife spent among the stars of the Milky Way. **Medicine men** explain dreams, treat illnesses with herbs and other medicines, and help ward off evil with knowledge and wisdom. They also help others find harmony in their lives and with the world around them.

The most important religious person in Cheyenne **culture** was Sweet Medicine, a Cheyenne **prophet** who traveled to Bear Butte in the Black Hills and returned with the Sacred Arrows. The most important Cheyenne religious event each year is the Renewal of the Sacred Arrows, taking place in the summer on the longest day of the year. The feathers of the arrows are replaced in the ceremony. During the rest of the year, a Cheyenne elder guards the Sacred Arrows.

When the Sutaio people merged with the Cheyennes long ago, they brought the Sacred Medicine Hat, another religious item of great importance. The Sacred Medicine Hat (sometimes called the Sacred

(Left) The painting and decorations on this buckskin Cheyenne medicine tepee have religious significance. *(Right)* This Cheyenne buffalo medicine hat was part of the medicine-hat rituals the Cheyennes learned from the Sutaios.

Buffalo Hat) is entrusted to the care of a respected elder of Sutaio tribal descent. The Sutaios also shared ceremonies that are important parts of Cheyenne life, including the Sun Dance ceremony and the teachings of the Sutaio prophet named Erect Horns.

CHEYENNE MODERN LIFE
CHAPTER 10

Today, both the Northern and Southern Cheyennes retain and practice many elements of their traditional life. They also share the responsibilities of maintaining and protecting important religious items between the two tribes. The Northern Cheyennes keep the Sacred Medicine Hat, while the Southern Cheyennes guard the Sacred Arrows. The two tribes keep in close contact with each other, visiting frequently and attending each other's ceremonies and powwows.

Many Cheyennes live and work in urban areas throughout the United States, but most continue to live on or near their reservations in Montana and Oklahoma, where their daily lives are very similar to those of other rural Americans.

Now that Cheyenne children are no longer sent away to boarding schools, they can live at home with their families and participate in powwows and other tribal activities. They now have educational opportunities that other children have while still being able to maintain their Cheyenne culture. Many Cheyennes have acquired college educations and pursue careers as managers, doctors, lawyers, and teachers.

Native American Dwight White Buffalo, a Cheyenne from Watonga, Oklahoma, dances at the National Powwow. Since judges watch many dancers compete at the same time, they track his performance by the number he is wearing.

THE NORTHERN CHEYENNE TODAY

CHAPTER 11

The Northern Cheyenne Reservation was increased to its present size of 444,500 acres (180,000 ha) in southeastern Montana by a presidential order in 1900. Bordered on the west by the Crow Reservation and on the east by the Tongue River, the reservation is home to about 6,000 of the approximately 8,000 tribal members.

While some of the land consists of steep hills and narrow valleys, much of the reservation is rich grassland and hills. Ranching and farming are the most important economic activities. The tribe also maintains herds of elk and buffalo. The Cheyenne buffalo herd was started in the 1970s and now numbers more than 100 animals on nearly 4,000 acres (1,600 ha) of grassland. The tribe also manages 90,000 acres (36,400 ha) of forests for harvesting and selling timber.

The Northern Cheyennes have refused to allow the mining of rich coal deposits, which were discovered in 1960, on their reservation. They object to the destruction of the land from open-pit mining, which occurs in areas near the reservation.

Cheyenne tepees stand near Lame Deer, Montana, in the Northern Cheyenne Reservation, a place of great natural beauty.

THE SOUTHERN CHEYENNE TODAY

CHAPTER 12

Since 1869, the Southern Cheyennes have been joined with the Southern Arapahos on the Concho Reservation on the edge of the Great Plains in western Oklahoma. Known as the Cheyenne-Arapaho Tribes of Oklahoma, the two tribes govern the reservation by a joint business committee composed of representatives elected from both tribes under a **constitution** adopted in 1937.

The original reservation consisted of more than 5 million acres (2,024,000 ha). Today, only 85,000 acres (34,400 ha) remain in tribal control. Most of the land that was individually assigned to tribal members in the late nineteenth century soon passed into white hands, often by **fraud**.

During the 1950s, the U.S. Bureau of Indian Affairs and the U.S. Congress attempted to end the status of the tribe as an independent nation.

Today, the combined population of the Southern Cheyennes and Southern Arapahos is about 10,000, of which about half live on the Concho Reservation. Many of the others live in Oklahoma City and other urban areas in the region.

Farming and cattle raising are important economic activities. A tribally owned **casino** provides both employment for tribal members and income for tribal programs, such as health care and education.

A Southern Cheyenne in traditional dress wears a headdress made of feathers.

CURRENT ISSUES

CHAPTER 13

Health issues are a big concern for the Cheyennes, with high suicide and diabetes rates. The tribes are also looking to improve education and transportation facilities.

One other issue has been ongoing for a very long time. Although the U.S. government promised the Cheyennes compensation for the Sand Creek Massacre as long ago as 1865, the tribes are still campaigning to have this money paid to them. Today the land in Eads, Colorado, is part of

Members of the Southern Cheyenne and Arapaho tribes march through Washington, D.C., during a celebration of Native American culture and identity.

the Sand Creek Massacre National Historic Site. In December 2014, people gathered to commemorate the lives lost 150 years earlier.

The Southern Cheyennes are beginning to build wind farms to make use of wind energy in Oklahoma. The first 22 **turbines**, built in 2011 and 2012, are designed to power the tribal headquarters, the tribal smoke shop, and a casino.

Both the Northern and Southern Cheyenne people are adjusting to the great changes they have endured during the past century. They are now taking control of their lives, rather than having their lives controlled by the U.S. government.

Turbines like the ones found on this Oklahoma wind farm turn energy from the wind into electricity.

GLOSSARY

alcoholism: A disease marked by overuse of alcohol, leading to other health problems.

alien: Unfamiliar, foreign.

allotment: The act of dividing land and forcing Native Americans to accept individual ownership of small farms, rather than all of the Indian land being owned by the tribe as a whole.

casino: A building where gambling takes place.

constitution: The basic laws and principles of a nation that outline the powers of the government and the rights of the people.

courtship: The act of courting, or trying to win the favor and love of a romantic partner.

culture: The arts, beliefs, and customs that form a people's way of life.

epidemic: A widespread outbreak of a serious disease.

fraud: An act of tricking or cheating.

immigrant: Someone who comes to a new place from another country.

light cavalry: Soldiers trained to fight on horseback.

massacre: The killing of many people.

medicine man: A religious leader and healer.

militia: A group of soldiers who come together in an emergency to protect their community.

nomadic: Having to do with nomads, or people who move from place to place.

poverty: The state of being poor.

powwow: A Native American ceremony that includes feasting, singing, and dancing.

prophet: Someone who is believed to be able to tell what will happen in the future.

reservation: Land set aside by the government for specific Native American tribes to live on.

tepee: A tent that is shaped like a cone and was used in the past by some Native Americans as a house.

treaty: An agreement among nations or people.

trespass: To enter someone's home or land without permission.

turbine: A motor operated by the movement of water, steam, or air.

whiskey: A strong alcoholic drink made from barley or rye.

FOR MORE INFORMATION

BOOKS

Lowery, Linda. *Native Peoples of the Plains.* Minneapolis, MN: Lerner Publications, 2015.

Marciniak, Kristin. *The Oregon Trail and Westward Expansion.* Ann Arbor, Michigan: Cherry Lake Publishing, 2013.

Tieck, Sarah. *Cheyenne.* Edina, MN: ABDO Publishing Company, 2015.

WEBSITES

Due to the changing nature of Internet links, PowerKids Press has developed an online list of websites related to the subject of this book. This site is updated regularly. Please use this link to access the list: www.powerkidslinks.com/sona/chey

INDEX